THE
BITCOIN
SUPERHEROES

What is Bitcoin?

MANDO CT

First published in Great Britain in 2025

Copyright © Mando CT

The moral right of the author has been asserted.

All rights reserved.

Editing, design, typesetting and publishing by UK Book Publishing.

www.ukbookpublishing.com

ISBN: 978-1-917329-60-6

Table of Contents

Dedication

Here's to my incredible wife and children. Most books begin with a dedication to friends and family, but I want to take a moment to express my deepest gratitude directly to you. Your unwavering support and belief in me have been the foundation of this work. Thank you for standing by me through every challenge and celebrating every success. This book is a testament to your love and encouragement.

    – Mando CT

Introduction

D o you remember when people used to dismiss the internet in the 1990s?

Bitcoin might be that next big technological revolution you don't want to overlook. It's undoubtedly one of the most groundbreaking innovations I've ever encountered. If you brush off learning about Bitcoin, you might end up like those who doubted the internet all those years ago.

People still label it a 'bubble', yet millions around the globe are adopting it, including major hedge funds, insurance companies, and notable investors like Donald Trump, Elon Musk, and many more.

In this guide, we'll explore the fundamentals that make Bitcoin one of the most profitable investments in history, potentially the most profitable. We'll also examine what drives a virtual currency to become the 21st century's Digital Gold.

Bitcoin is a topic most people don't grasp. Many will read a few headlines and draw their own conclusions; this is the wrong way to understand Bitcoin.

Drawing on everything I've learned from my mentor and from some of the brightest minds in this space, "The Bitcoin Superheroes", this guide has been designed to take you from knowing nothing about Bitcoin to:

- Understanding what Bitcoin actually is
- Discovering its many use cases
- Grasping why investors are so keen on this emerging asset

What's included:
- A beginner-friendly explanation
- Bitcoin's fundamentals
- Why it's an opportunity
- Bitcoin's future
- Possible risks

Common criticisms
1. How to invest
2. How to buy
3. How to store
4. Earning interest
5. The macroeconomics behind Bitcoin
6. Extra resources for further learning

If you've been waiting for your chance to invest in Bitcoin, now might be the moment.

Let's remember Warren Buffett's quote: "Risk comes from not knowing what you're doing." That's precisely why it's crucial to understand what we're investing in.

I need you to take your time and go step by step. This approach will help you make the most of the information I'll be sharing here. Don't compete with anyone, don't rush, and think long-term.

"All strategies and investments involve the risk of loss. No information contained in this product should be understood as a guarantee of results."

Who Am I?

I grew up in Liverpool, UK, in a humble home where talk of "riches" felt like a distant dream. Yet, from an early age, I couldn't shake the feeling that life held more possibilities than what I saw around me. When I was older, I spent 15 years in traditional finance, travelling, learning how money really moves, and pushing myself beyond every comfort zone I had.

But it wasn't until 2016, in a moment of curiosity, that I stumbled upon Bitcoin. Let's be honest: I had no idea what I was getting into. At the time, Bitcoin seemed like an odd invention. Still, something about it, its decentralised nature, its promise of a new financial frontier, pulled me in. I started small, buying just a few coins, studying the technology late into the night, and watching that price chart zigzag in ways I'd never seen in typical markets.

Soon, I found myself going deeper, taking classes, meeting people who lived and breathed crypto, and absorbing every bit of knowledge I could. I also made mistakes. There were wild market swings, and times when I doubted if I'd made the right choice. But each setback pushed me to learn more. In fact, I've lost thousands of pounds in trades, only to discover new strategies and insights on the rebound.

Over time, I realised Bitcoin wasn't just another investment. It was changing how I viewed money, risk, and opportunity. My fascination turned into a full-time commitment, and I began sharing what I knew on social media. The crypto world can be chaotic, but it's also brimming with innovators and dreamers, precisely the environment I thrive in.

Why Write a Book on Bitcoin?

I'm not here to convince you to buy Bitcoin. I'd rather help you understand *why* millions of people, from hedge funds to small-scale investors, are pouring into this space. After reading, I hope you'll form your own opinion based on a solid grasp of the fundamentals.

A Quick Disclaimer

This guide is a starting point, not the final word. I'm not a financial adviser, and any information here should be viewed in light of your own situation. No investment is guaranteed, past successes don't promise future results. Always consult a professional before making big decisions.

With that in mind, let's dive into the world of Bitcoin and see why it's captured so many imaginations. It's been a wild ride for me, full of highs, lows, and everything in between. I invite you to join me on this adventure, because if there's one thing I know, it's that the crypto landscape never stands still. Let's explore what Bitcoin can do for you and, just as importantly, for the world around us.

What is Bitcoin?

I s it money? A Ponzi Scheme? A store of value? Or just some bits on a computer?

Bitcoin is a digital currency, or cryptocurrency, created in 2009 by an anonymous person, or group, using the pseudonym Satoshi Nakamoto. Because nobody knows exactly who created Bitcoin, it operates as a fully decentralised currency, with no Central Bank in control.

With Bitcoin, there's no need to rely on a third party, and users can make transactions without interference from governments or other entities.

In short, Bitcoin is a digital form of money.

How does Bitcoin operate?

Bitcoin runs on open-source software, so anyone can look into how it works and see what transactions have taken place at any time. These transactions are stored on an immutable – meaning it cannot be altered – public ledger known as the *blockchain*.

These transactions are verified by "miners". Miners use computing power to solve complex mathematical problems in order to validate these transactions.

The first miner to solve the problem broadcasts the transactions to the ledger (the distributed ledger), but only if at least 51% of other miners confirm the transactions are correct. Because the mining network is decentralised and there are many miners around the world, it's very unlikely that fraudulent transactions get verified. So if any "bad actor" attempts to submit fraudulent transactions, they'll waste their computing power, as the network won't confirm them.

Miners want to earn rewards for their work, which motivates them to only record transactions that have actually occurred on the network.

This transaction verification process is called "Proof of Work", and it still functions seamlessly today.

Ownership

Each Bitcoin user has a public key and a private key. The public key is the one everyone on the network can see on the blockchain.

To use your home as an analogy, the public key would be similar to your house address. A private key is what you use to transact with Bitcoin from the address linked to your public key. In this analogy, the private key is the key you use to unlock the door.

Everyone can know your public address, but nobody should ever have access to your private key. If someone does get hold of your private key, they effectively have access to your Bitcoin.

If you store your Bitcoin on an exchange, you don't need to manage a private key yourself, as it's held in the Exchange's Wallet. I'll go into more detail on how to store your Bitcoin in the next sections.

What about printing?

The interesting thing about Bitcoin is that there will only ever be 21 million coins in total. Each Bitcoin can be split into 100 million individual units, known as "satoshis". This means you don't need to buy an entire coin; you could buy just a dollar's worth if you wanted to. Thanks to this high divisibility, Bitcoin can be used for smaller transactions.

Given that the supply cap stands at 21 million, this makes Bitcoin the first asset ever created with a hard limit on how many units can be produced.

It's truly a finite resource.

Because of its fixed supply, Bitcoin is a viable option for people experiencing currency collapses in their country. These sorts of countries often have governments that overreach in terms of capital controls.

Bitcoin can act as an "escape" from a failing currency because, unlike gold or real estate, it cannot be seized.

Historically, gold was used as the primary form of money before fiat currencies (dollar, euro, pound, etc.) took over, but even gold does not have a strict supply limit. Over the past century, miners have managed to produce about 1.5–2.0% more gold each year.

Since this new flow of gold supply was relatively low compared to other forms of money, people naturally adopted it as a fiat currency alternative; it managed to hold its value over time.

When the price of gold rises, it encourages gold miners to extract more, which increases the overall supply and can exert downward pressure on the price. If the price of gold suddenly doubled from $2,000 to $4,000 per ounce, miners would do everything possible to pull out more gold, effectively diluting its overall supply.

With Bitcoin, no matter how high the price goes, the same number of units is added to the network. That's because it is programmed to have a maximum supply of 21 million coins.

This is a crucial aspect of what Bitcoin represents. More shares can be created (like a stock split), more gold can be mined, more dollars can be printed, but there will never be more than 21 million Bitcoins.

Assuming it continues to have stable or growing demand, this makes it highly resistant to inflation and arguably the strongest form of money that could exist.

What about censorship?

In addition to solving the issue of monetary scarcity, Bitcoin also addresses the problem of censorship. It's the first digital payment method that does not rely on a middleman to function.

Today, governments and banks have the power to block transactions between individuals for various reasons. Censorship might start out with good intentions, but it can eventually reach a point where these entities impose it for their own benefit rather than society's greater good.

Bitcoin allows transactions to happen freely between any two people. It grants individual and complete control over your money.

What about transferring?

Sending cross-border payments can often be quite expensive, another problem Bitcoin solves. Transferring funds internationally through traditional banking systems can be costly and time-consuming, often involving significant transaction fees and delays of several days. Bitcoin addresses these challenges by enabling users to send funds across borders with minimal fees and near-instantaneous processing times.

As of early January 2025, the average transaction fee on the Bitcoin network is approximately $1.40, reflecting a decrease from previous months.

Additionally, the average confirmation time for Bitcoin transactions is around 29.73 minutes as of January 5, 2025.

These improvements enhance Bitcoin's appeal as a cost-effective and efficient solution for cross-border payments.

In fact, one of the largest transactions ever recorded was 161,500 Bitcoins, worth approximately $4.4 billion at the time, sent at a cost of just $0.40 in transaction fees. (Source: Blockchain.com)

Bitcoin is the first technology ever created that allows its users to transfer value across both space and time without a significant loss of purchasing power. In theory, it does not lose its purchasing power over time because it's not diluted by the introduction of new units into the total supply. It's a global network requiring no one's approval.

Bitcoin knows no borders.

According to Robert Breedlove's article, "An Open Letter to Ray Dalio", market participants have historically adopted a form of money that naturally exhibits the following five properties:

1. **Scarcity:** Resistant to manipulations of the monetary supply and, therefore, dilution of its unit value (difficult to produce).
2. **Divisibility:** Ease of accounting and transactions on various scales (units can be separated and combined).
3. **Portability:** Ease of moving value across space (high value-to-weight ratio).
4. **Durability:** Ease of moving value across time (resistant to deterioration).
5. **Recognition:** Ease of identifying and verifying monetary value by other parties in a transaction (universally recognisable and verifiable).

Below is a table showing how gold, government money (fiat money), and Bitcoin rank in these categories.

Characteristics	Gold	Government Money	Bitcoin
Scarcity	Medium	Low	High
Divisibility	Low	Medium	High
Portability	Medium	High	High
Durability	High	Medium	High
Recognition	Medium	High	High

Bitcoin as an Opportunity

Owing to its favourable monetary properties, Bitcoin has seen tremendous adoption and price growth. Here is a log chart as of 21 December 2024:

In the following example, we'll compare Bitcoin to two of the most common investments people make in the markets: Gold and the S&P 500.

Now let's create a table to see the impact of our supposed investment from 21 November 2011 until early 2025:

Asset	21/11/2011	03/01/2025 Approx.	Growth
Bitcoin	$2.30	$94,350.39	4,264,226.09%
Gold	$1,678.30	$2,687.93	15.00%
S&P 500	$1,192.98	$5,827.04	285.58%

Source: https://www.investing.com/

With these returns, we can calculate how much a $100 investment in each of them might have yielded, held from 21 November 2011 to the present day:

Bitcoin:
- $100 at $2.30 per Bitcoin would have bought 43.48 BTC. 43.48 BTC at today's price of $94,350.39 would be worth $4,103,529.74 (the amount is extraordinary).

You can see the rest for yourself, but the difference is staggering. Very few assets – only Bitcoin – really, would have made us millionaires from an investment of just $100 in those 13 years.

With the price increases over the years, Bitcoin's total market capitalisation currently sits at around $1.84 trillion as of January 2025. Gold's current market capitalisation stands at approximately $13 trillion, which is about seven times larger than Bitcoin.

Because of its superior monetary attributes, many believe Bitcoin's market capitalisation will eventually surpass that of gold. Thus, even at current prices, Bitcoin still offers significant growth potential for investors.

The massive price rise is due to two main factors:

1. An exponentially growing number of users.
2. A decreasing flow of new supply.

1) User Growth

The price of Bitcoin and the number of active wallets can indeed be correlated, though it's important to note that correlation does not necessarily imply causation. When Bitcoin's price rises, it often attracts more attention, leading to an increase in wallet activity, whether it's from new users entering the market or existing users trading more frequently.

Several factors could be at play here:

1. Increased interest with rising prices: As the price of Bitcoin increases, it garners more media attention, attracting more users to create wallets and engage in trading.
2. Speculation and investment: People might open new wallets and become more active in response to price speculation, looking to profit from price movements.
3. Market psychology: As Bitcoin rises in price, it often triggers a "fear of missing out" (FOMO), which can lead to more people getting involved in the market, increasing the number of active wallets.

However, it's worth noting that wallet activity can also be influenced by other factors, like improvements in infrastructure, institutional involvement, or global economic events. Therefore, while there seems to be a correlation, it's a complex relationship with multiple influencing variables.

The rising number of users results from network effects built up over the past decade. Bitcoin was the first successful cryptocurrency ever created.

When most people hear the word "cryptocurrency", the first one they think of is Bitcoin.

The following have contributed to the network's growth:

- It has been regulated by governments as an asset, with regulated exchanges.

- It has been the best-performing asset over the last decade.
- Its rapid appreciation has drawn more and more investors who want to learn about it.

It's easy to underestimate the power that's gathered around it.

Likewise, what happened with telephone networks, the internet, Facebook, Google, etc., is likely to happen with Bitcoin via network effects.

As the asset gains strength and renown in the market, it becomes harder for competitors to knock it off its podium.

Theoretically, anyone can copy its code, but they cannot copy the mining network, the exchanges that trade it, the people who view it as an investment, the developers working on the network, and so on.

Another underappreciated element is how difficult it is to disrupt a monetary network. When a wealthy individual decides to invest billions in Bitcoin, that has an exponential effect compared to the growth of other networks. As Michael Saylor put it, "Nobody brings a thousand million friends to Facebook."

Major institutions have also become interested in Bitcoin. A Citibank report published in November 2020 predicted a price above $300,000 by December 2021.

In October 2020, PayPal enabled customers to buy, hold, and sell cryptocurrencies for its 300 million users, instantly allowing people to purchase without having to research which exchange to use.

(Note: I do not recommend buying Bitcoin on PayPal. Here's an article explaining why: https://boingboing.net/2020/11/12/beware-of-buying-cryptocurrency-on-paypal.html)

Investors have recently shown more interest due to Bitcoin's unique qualities as a store of value that protects against inflation.

Data reveals that over 60% of Bitcoin in existence today hasn't moved in more than a year.

This suggests that many holders see it as a store of wealth, holding it rather than using it for everyday transactions.

Even insurance companies have begun investing in Bitcoin.

In December 2020, Massachusetts Mutual Life Insurance announced it had purchased $100 million in Bitcoin.

This opens the door for other insurers seeking higher returns on their investments.

Major companies have also started adopting it on their balance sheets.

MicroStrategy, a prominent business intelligence firm, has significantly increased its Bitcoin holdings. As of January 5, 2025, the company owns approximately 447,470 bitcoins, acquired at an aggregate purchase price of about $27.97 billion, averaging $62,503 per bitcoin.

In late December 2024, MicroStrategy purchased an additional 1,070 bitcoins for $101 million, at an average price of $94,004 per bitcoin. This acquisition underscores the company's ongoing commitment to Bitcoin as a primary treasury reserve asset.

Square, headed by Twitter CEO Jack Dorsey, also revealed a $50 million position in October 2020, which represents around 1% of its total treasury.

If Bitcoin continues to succeed, I believe more companies will follow suit and include it in their reserves.

2) Decreasing Supply Flow.

Its price isn't just rising due to growing demand; it's also doing so as a result of a declining flow of new supply.

Once again, the total supply is capped at 21 million coins.

Currently, there are about 18.5 million in circulation, and 100% of the coins are expected to be mined by the year 2140.

The reason it takes so long for the remaining coins to be mined is that the block reward given to miners halves every four years. This means supply is added at a decreasing rate.

The reward for miners currently stands at 6.25 BTC per block, and this reward is halved approximately every four years during the Bitcoin halving events. The next halving is expected to occur in 2024, at which point the block reward will decrease to 3.125 BTC.

Here's a breakdown of the halving impact:

- Currently (2020–2024): 6.25 BTC rewarded every 10 minutes, leading to 900 BTC per day.
- Post-2024 Halving: 3.125 BTC rewarded every 10 minutes, leading to 450 BTC per day.

The halving process is important because it reduces the rate at which new Bitcoin is introduced into circulation. This is a key aspect of Bitcoin's monetary policy, and it has historically led to price increases, largely due to reduced supply combined with steady or increasing demand. The decrease in rewards also means that miners will need to rely more on transaction fees for their income, particularly if the block reward decreases enough that it doesn't sufficiently cover mining costs.

The halving event typically results in a lot of market attention, as many anticipate that the reduction in the rate of new Bitcoin entering circulation may lead to upward pressure on the price, assuming demand remains steady or grows.

This cut in incoming supply has had a major impact on price movements.

Let's look at the following model created by an anonymous Twitter account, which proposes a forecasting model called *Stock-to-Flow* to predict future movements.

An anonymous Twitter user called **PlanB** [@100trillionUSD] developed a **Stock-to-Flow** model that predicts future price movements.

Historically, the Stock-to-Flow ratio has been useful for determining what makes a good store of value. "Stock" refers to the total existing supply of the asset, and "Flow" refers to the new units produced over a certain period.

To determine the Stock-to-Flow ratio, you simply take inventory divided by flow. An asset with a high Stock-to-Flow ratio (such as gold) has historically served as a solid store of value because new incoming supply doesn't significantly affect the total supply.

The chart below shows Bitcoin's price performance relative to the price predicted by the Stock-to-Flow model. The white line represents the model's projected value, which shifts significantly on the day the supply flow is halved. The coloured dots on the chart represent monthly closing prices.

Table 1: Stock-to-Flow Ratios (PlanB Data)

Asset	Stock (Existing Supply)	Flow (Annual Production)	S2F Ratio
Bitcoin	19.5M BTC	~328,500 BTC	59
Gold	205,000 tonnes	3,300 tonnes	62
Silver	1,740,000 tonnes	26,000 tonnes	22

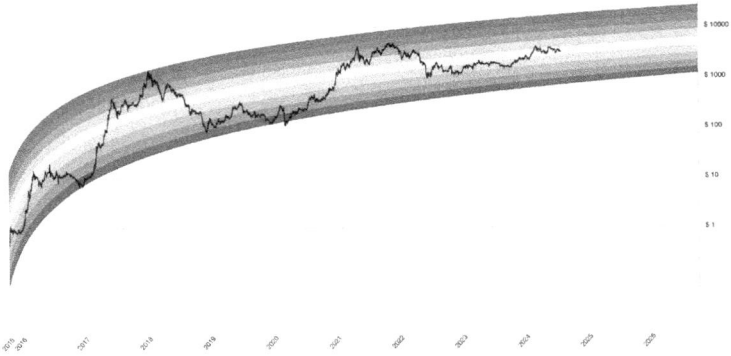

As you can see, the model has so far been surprisingly accurate with the price. After each halving, the price adjusts towards a new equilibrium based on the reduced supply flow.

This model suggests that price is greatly influenced by the new flow, which is cut in half every four years.

Bitcoin's S2F ratio (existing supply divided by annual production) increases after each halving, making it scarcer than gold (see Table 1).

Despite volatility, Bitcoin's price has closely tracked the S2F model over time. Major bull markets (2013, 2017, 2021) align with post-halving supply shocks, while bear markets occur when price overshoots the model (e.g., 2014, 2018).

The next halving (April 2024) will reduce annual supply to 0.8% of the total stock, pushing Bitcoin's S2F ratio to 112 – higher than gold's 60 – and further validating the model's long-term trajectory. Bitcoin Drawdowns & Recovery Cycles (2013–2023) [Insert a chart showing major drawdowns (e.g., -80% in 2018, -65% in 2022) and subsequent recoveries to new all-time highs. Highlight how each cycle took less time to rebound.] Key points to emphasize: No broken cycles: Despite drops of 70–80%, Bitcoin has always recovered, with each bear market floor higher than the previous cycle's peak (e.g., 2017 peak: 20k→2021peak:69k). S2F alignment: Recoveries align with the "accumulation" phase of the S2F model, where price trades below predicted value before surging post-halving.

Bitcoin's S2F ratio is already comparable to gold's, but post-2024 halving, it will dwarf all traditional commodities, cementing its "digital gold" narrative.

It's important to remember that miners are continuous sellers of Bitcoin because they usually pay their electricity bills in fiat currency.

You can read more about PlanB's work here:

https://100trillionusd.github.io

The Stock-to-Flow model predicts a price of $100,000 by the end of 2021. There are several variations of the model, one of which forecasts a price of $288,000 for the same period.

PlanB's Stock-to-Flow (S2F) model is an interesting approach to valuing Bitcoin by comparing its scarcity to other assets like gold. The Stock-to-Flow ratio is calculated by dividing the current stock (total supply of an asset) by the flow (new units produced or mined each year). The higher the ratio, the more scarce the asset is considered, since it would take longer to replace the existing supply with new production.

Current Stock-to-Flow of Bitcoin and Gold:

- Bitcoin's current Stock-to-Flow ratio: Around 53.
- This means it would take about 53 years to produce the same amount of Bitcoin as currently exists at the current

production rate (6.25 BTC per block, halving every four years).

- Gold's current Stock-to-Flow ratio: Higher than Bitcoin's at around 60–70.
- Gold is historically seen as a store of value, largely due to its high stock-to-flow ratio.
- After the 2024 Halving:
- The block reward for miners will be halved from 6.25 BTC to 3.125 BTC, reducing the new supply of Bitcoin significantly.
- Bitcoin's Stock-to-Flow ratio will increase, and it will surpass gold's ratio after the 2024 halving, making Bitcoin the scarcity leader among major assets.

This increased scarcity (via the rising Stock-to-Flow ratio) could fuel more demand, as many believe that as an asset becomes scarcer, its price may rise due to a supply-demand imbalance, assuming demand remains steady or increases.

Potential Impact:

- Price Potential: Historically, the Stock-to-Flow model has been used to predict the potential future price of Bitcoin. As the halving increases Bitcoin's scarcity, it could lead to higher prices over time, similar to previous halvings.
- Market Sentiment: This rising scarcity and the potential for higher future prices could attract more investors who view Bitcoin as a hedge against inflation, or as a digital alternative to gold.

However, it's important to recognize that the S2F model, while compelling, isn't foolproof. There are other factors, such as regulatory developments, technological advancements, and macroeconomic conditions, that can affect Bitcoin's price and adoption.

Mining Difficulty (Hash Rate)

This hasn't come up yet in this guide, but as more miners join the network, the complex mathematical problem they solve becomes more difficult due to heightened competition for the block reward.

Because the puzzle is more difficult, more computing power is needed to solve it. This makes the network more secure, as fraudulent transactions become harder to pull off.

The hash rate measures how much work a miner has to do to validate transactions on the ledger and solve the complicated puzzle. The higher the hash rate, the more challenging it is to compromise the network, and the more secure it becomes.

In the next chart, we can see how, as the hash rate has increased, so too has the price. However, it's not the only indicator that might drive the asset's price upward, but it's certainly one of them.

Historically, the hash rate has been a useful metric for validating the "health" of the Bitcoin network.

The Future of Bitcoin

So far, Bitcoin has appeared to be a self-fulfilling prophecy.

1. **As the price increases,**
2. **This makes mining more profitable.**
3. **If mining is more profitable, miners will invest in new, more efficient platforms.**
4. **With investment in new mining platforms, the network as a whole becomes more secure as a payment network.**
5. **With a more secure network, market participants view Bitcoin as a more attractive investment.**

This cycle has repeated itself time and again.

Bitcoin has successfully established itself within the financial sector and has paved the way for large companies and influential individuals to engage and take a position. Therefore, one could argue that some portion of any portfolio should be allocated to Bitcoin. Whether it's 1%, 5%, 10%, etc., depends on the individual's conviction and risk tolerance.

If its astronomical growth continues, it would be wise to have at least some exposure to the asset. To put into perspective what this could do for your portfolio, if you allocate just 1% to Bitcoin and 99% to cash, the returns would surpass those of the S&P 500 (based on past performance).

Let's Talk About Volatility

Bitcoin has historically been known for its high volatility, with significant price swings over both short and long periods. These large downturns, which are often called "market corrections", have been part of Bitcoin's market behaviour, particularly during the early years of its existence.

Key Points Regarding Bitcoin's Volatility:

1. Significant Price Swings: Bitcoin has seen numerous periods of rapid price increases followed by dramatic corrections. These downturns are often fuelled by changes in investor sentiment, regulatory news, technological advancements, or macroeconomic factors. For example, Bitcoin saw massive volatility during events such as:
   - The 2017 bull run, followed by a sharp decline in 2018.
   - The crash in March 2020, when Bitcoin's price fell sharply due to the onset of the COVID-19 pandemic.

2. Volatility as Part of Its Nature: Given Bitcoin's relatively small market capitalization compared to traditional assets like gold or stocks, its price can be more sensitive to market sentiment. This can cause rapid fluctuations in its price, especially when large investors (whales) or institutions make significant moves in the market.

3. Historical Downturns: Looking at Bitcoin's largest downturns in its history (after 2013), we see dramatic losses in value after each significant bull run, including:

    - The 2011 crash (from around $31 to as low as $2).
    - The 2013-2015 crash (from about $1,150 to roughly $200).
    - The 2017-2018 crash (from nearly $20,000 to below $4,000).
    - The March 2020 COVID-19-induced crash (from around $9,100 to $4,200).

    Despite these downturns, Bitcoin has always managed to recover and set new highs, contributing to its long-term growth trajectory.

4. The Impact of Volatility: For investors, the volatility presents both a risk and an opportunity. Some investors might use market downturns to buy Bitcoin at lower prices, while others may get spooked and sell during corrections.

5. Long-Term Outlook: While Bitcoin's volatility has been a hallmark feature of its history, many proponents view the asset as having strong long-term potential, especially with increasing institutional involvement and its limited supply. For those who are able to ride out the volatility, Bitcoin has proven to be a highly rewarding investment over the long run.

Could the Volatility Continue?

Given Bitcoin's still-evolving market, it's likely that significant volatility will persist, especially during periods of global uncertainty or market speculation. However, as Bitcoin becomes more widely adopted, it may start to stabilize somewhat, though it will likely always be more volatile compared to traditional assets.

Positive Implications

First and foremost, it's important to acknowledge that regulations surrounding cryptocurrencies vary significantly across the world, with many governments still defining how to handle them.

Bitcoin's decentralised nature offers an alternative to traditional financial systems, granting users greater control over their assets. This makes Bitcoin particularly attractive as a store of value and a hedge against economic instability.

Its finite supply and resistance to external interference position Bitcoin as a unique financial tool. Unlike fiat currencies, which can be subject to inflationary pressures, Bitcoin's capped supply ensures scarcity, which many believe could drive its value in the long term.

This global asset also enables seamless, borderless transactions, giving people the freedom to move value without restrictions or intermediaries. As adoption increases, the possibilities for Bitcoin's integration into everyday financial systems continue to grow.

It's essential to stay informed about the landscape of cryptocurrencies in your region and make decisions based on your individual goals and risk tolerance. Bitcoin represents a new frontier in finance, and understanding its potential is key to leveraging it effectively.

Is Bitcoin Legal?

I'll provide a series of examples from European countries in line with the audience this guide is aimed at.

Very few countries have declared it illegal. So far, only Japan has granted it that designation. However, the fact that something isn't legal tender doesn't mean it can't be used as a payment method, it simply means there are no protections for either the consumer or the merchant, and its use as payment is entirely discretionary.

A clarification before presenting the examples: most governments are "afraid" of it, as this asset empowers individuals, and therefore, they tend to discourage its use.

United Kingdom

According to the UK's financial regulations, Bitcoin is not considered legal tender because it is not issued by the Bank of England. Despite its strong ecosystem, the UK has yet to develop comprehensive regulations for cryptocurrency, although the Financial Conduct Authority (FCA) has issued official warnings about the associated risks.

Germany

In Germany, Bitcoin is recognised as private money. This means it is not legal tender, but it can be used for transactions without restriction. The FCA regulates cryptocurrency exchanges, ensuring a degree of security for users.

France

France treats Bitcoin as an asset rather than currency. Transactions using Bitcoin are subject to capital gains tax if they result in a profit.

The government has implemented measures to prevent money laundering and terrorist financing through cryptocurrency.

Europe

In April 2018, European Parliament members voted overwhelmingly in favour of the December 2017 agreement with the European Council on measures aimed, in part, at preventing the use of cryptocurrencies for money laundering and the financing of terrorism. In early 2020, the 5th Anti-Money Laundering Directive (5AMLD) was enacted, placing cryptocurrency service providers under greater scrutiny.

Switzerland

Switzerland is known for its progressive stance on cryptocurrency. Bitcoin is recognised as an asset class, and the country has established itself as a crypto-friendly hub with clear regulations and supportive infrastructure.

For more information about your respective country, I recommend searching on sites related to the world of cryptocurrencies.

Personally, I know people from all over Europe using and trading Bitcoin regularly, so I encourage you to explore it further.

Macroeconomics

We live in a world where almost everyone thinks short-term. People are addicted to alcohol, fast food, sugar, and cheap dopamine. Many live pay cheque to pay cheque and become insolvent almost immediately if they lose their job.

Savings rates continue to decline, and all forms of debt keep rising. This is partly because fiat currencies do not retain their value. Since fiat currencies lose value over time, people are incentivised to think short-term and have a low temporal preference.

When the world was on the gold standard, people had much longer time horizons and could rely on their money retaining value as savings.

When the United Kingdom was on the gold standard, money was backed by gold, which limited the amount of new money that could be printed. Since fiat money is no longer backed by anything, there is no limit to how much money the Bank of England can print. Fiat money is only backed by society's belief in its monetary value.

The pound or euro are only sources of "savings" and "store of value" in countries where currencies are even worse. A well-known case is Venezuela, where the money is worth less than toilet paper, thanks to leaders who know little or nothing about economics.

Risks

Any investment with potential benefits comes with its fair share of risks. Bitcoin has only existed for 12 years and still needs time to mature and be adopted by the conventional financial system. Potential headwinds may include, but are not limited to:

- **Regulatory Pressures:** Attempts to ban Bitcoin or make it illegal to buy and sell.
- **Technical Vulnerabilities:** If there is a flaw in the code, it could potentially lead to a network collapse. However, Bitcoin has operated smoothly so far, but that does not mean that something unexpected cannot occur in the future with the protocol.
- **Emergence of Superior Assets:** A new emerging asset that surpasses the influence Bitcoin has established.
- **Government Fiscal Responsibility:** Governments around the world becoming fiscally responsible, making the transition to cryptocurrencies unnecessary.

It is essential to be aware of these risks and conduct thorough research before making any investment decisions.

Common Criticisms

"Bitcoin Has No Intrinsic Value"

Many people are sceptical and will say it's a bubble or that it has no intrinsic value. This is understandable if you don't fully grasp what has driven Bitcoin's adoption and how it compares to other bubbles throughout history.

Bitcoin's ability to recover from previous downturns is indeed one of its standout characteristics, especially when compared to historical financial bubbles like Tulip Mania, the South Sea Bubble, and the Dot-Com Bubble. Let's dive into the resilience of Bitcoin in relation to these famous bubbles.

Comparing Bitcoin to Historical Bubbles:

1. Tulip Mania (1634-1637):
    *   Event: Considered one of the first speculative bubbles, where the price of tulip bulbs in the Netherlands skyrocketed before collapsing.
    *   Outcome: After the bubble burst, the tulip market never recovered to its previous heights, and it became a cautionary tale for speculative investments.
    *   Bitcoin Comparison: Bitcoin has undergone several boom-bust cycles but has repeatedly managed to recover and surpass previous all-time highs, showing a long-term upward trend despite extreme volatility.

2. South Sea Company (1719-1722):

- Event: The South Sea Company was a British trading company whose stock price was driven up by speculation. Eventually, the stock crashed, devastating investors.
- Outcome: The company never regained its previous peak value, and many investors lost their fortunes.
- Bitcoin Comparison: While Bitcoin has seen similar speculative behaviour, its underlying value proposition as a decentralized, scarce digital asset has allowed it to bounce back each time, continuing to attract new users and institutional investors.

3. Dot-Com Bubble (1994-2003):

- Event: The dot-com bubble involved the overvaluation of internet-based companies in the late 1990s. When the bubble burst, many of these companies crashed.
- Outcome: The companies that survived the crash (like Amazon, Google, and eBay) went on to become giants. However, many others disappeared, and investors who held the wrong stocks saw significant losses.
- Bitcoin Comparison: Bitcoin shares some similarities with the dot-com bubble, where early speculative fervour could have been seen as unsustainable. However, Bitcoin has demonstrated resilience through a decentralized network, a strong

community, and growing institutional interest, unlike the companies of the dot-com era, which had varying business models that didn't prove sustainable.

Why Bitcoin is Resilient:

1. Decentralization: Bitcoin's decentralized nature means that it's not reliant on any single company, government, or institution to survive. Even after significant downturns, the network itself remains intact, and the protocol continues to function.
2. Scarcity and Fixed Supply: Bitcoin's fixed supply (21 million BTC) creates an inherent scarcity, which increases its appeal as a store of value. This contrasts with the companies involved in bubbles, which could issue more shares or expand beyond sustainable growth.
3. Growing Institutional Adoption: Unlike the speculative bubbles of the past, Bitcoin is increasingly being embraced by institutional investors, which adds legitimacy and long-term viability to its value proposition.
4. Technological Advances: Bitcoin continues to evolve through developments like the Lightning Network and other improvements in scalability and security. This ongoing innovation supports its long-term viability.
5. Global Awareness and Demand: As more individuals and companies become aware of Bitcoin, demand has steadily increased. Bitcoin has crossed critical milestones of adoption, and it's viewed by many as a hedge against

inflation and a store of value, especially in uncertain economic climates.

Final Thoughts:

While Bitcoin has faced extreme volatility and large downturns, it has shown an ability to recover and push to new heights. The key difference between Bitcoin and historical bubbles is that Bitcoin is built on a decentralized and robust network with real utility, whereas the assets involved in past bubbles lacked such intrinsic value or long-term utility.

Bitcoin's resilience speaks to its ability to weather speculative storms, and while it may face further corrections, its unique characteristics may help it continue to recover and grow in the future.

If Bitcoin had no intrinsic value or use, I don't believe you would see interest from Wall Street and public companies wanting to hold it as a treasury reserve asset.

It is rumoured that Elon Musk might transfer Tesla's reserves to Bitcoin.

Saying it has no intrinsic value is simply not true. If you want to send money to anyone around the world almost instantly, Bitcoin is the only affordable way to do so. It takes many days to achieve this using fiat money through the banking system or by using gold. Bitcoin offers an incredibly affordable and efficient method to transfer value globally.

"Bitcoin Will Be Banned"

This could be one of the most common criticisms. It's misleading to think, "If Bitcoin succeeds, then it's inevitable that governments will simply ban it."

Bitcoin is, in fact, open-source software that can be used anywhere in the world (similar to the Internet). Because it is open-source, it is effectively protected by free speech laws (e.g., the First Amendment in the United States).

If free speech laws were somehow revoked (which is practically impossible to enforce), it would be similar to attempting to shut down the Internet globally.

Governments could block access to exchanges, but this would incentivise other countries to attract these companies to receive the tax revenues they generate.

"Bitcoin Is Too Concentrated"

Some people worry that Bitcoin is too concentrated in the hands of a few. Data suggests that 2,300 wallets hold 40% of the total supply. Though this doesn't account for exchanges that hold Bitcoin on behalf of others or wallets that have been lost.

On the other hand, Bitcoin wasn't created to solve wealth distribution. There have been disparities in wealth levels across all societies, and Bitcoin is no exception to this. With the way the current fiat system operates, money printing leads to asset inflation, which increases wealth inequality between the rich and the poor.

Bitcoin returns power to the people in the fairest possible way. Anyone can participate in this economy with the confidence that they won't be undermined by a third-party entity.

It also levels the playing field in many ways.

Why Are Elon Musk and Donald Trump So Important for the Cryptocurrency Community?

As you know, cryptocurrencies are becoming more and more trendy, and having influential people like these two interacting with bitcoin makes it even more viral. Elon Musk and Donald Trump have become significant figures in the Bitcoin world for various reasons, each bringing their unique influence and shaping the broader landscape of cryptocurrency adoption.

Elon Musk's Influence

Elon Musk, the visionary behind Tesla and SpaceX, plays a pivotal role in the cryptocurrency scene. His actions can create major shifts in Bitcoin's price and public perception.

When Tesla invested $1.5 billion in Bitcoin and started accepting it as payment for their cars in early 2021, it wasn't just a business decision, it was a powerful endorsement that boosted Bitcoin's legitimacy and value. Although Tesla later paused Bitcoin payments, citing environmental concerns, the initial move highlighted the potential for major companies to embrace cryptocurrencies seriously.

Musk's influence extends beyond his corporate ventures. Through his active presence on X (formerly Twitter), he has popularised not only Bitcoin but also other cryptocurrencies like Dogecoin. A single tweet from Musk can send Bitcoin's price soaring or plummeting within hours. Whether he's praising Dogecoin as the "people's cryptocurrency" or raising concerns about Bitcoin's energy consumption, his statements have immediate and substantial effects on the market.

Moreover, Musk is a strong advocate for technological innovation. His interest in decentralised finance (DeFi) and blockchain technology encourages both developers and investors to explore new opportunities within the crypto world. By supporting these advancements, Musk fosters a culture of growth and experimentation, pushing the boundaries of what's possible in the digital economy.

Donald Trump's Role

Donald Trump, the 45th and 47th President of the United States, has also left a notable mark on the cryptocurrency landscape, though in a different way compared to Elon Musk. His influence primarily comes from his administration's policies and regulatory approaches, which have shaped the environment in which cryptocurrencies operate.

During his first presidency, Trump maintained a cautious stance towards cryptocurrencies. While he didn't actively promote digital currencies, his administration focused on regulating them to prevent illicit activities such as money laundering and fraud. These regulatory efforts aimed to bring more transparency and accountability to the crypto market, encouraging the industry to adopt stricter compliance measures. Although some viewed these regulations as hurdles, they were essential steps towards legitimising cryptocurrencies as mainstream financial instruments.

Trump's public statements about the economy and financial policies often touched on cryptocurrencies, influencing how people and investors perceive digital currencies. By emphasising financial security and regulation, his administration affected investor confidence and market stability. Additionally, Trump's policies had global implications, influencing how other countries approached crypto regulations based on the precedents set by the US. This international ripple effect underscores the significant role political leaders play in shaping the global cryptocurrency ecosystem.

Comparing Their Impacts

While both Elon Musk and Donald Trump wield considerable influence over the cryptocurrency community, their impacts are quite different in nature and scope.

Elon Musk's influence is immediate and direct. His social media posts and business decisions can cause swift changes in cryptocurrency prices, affecting investor behaviour almost instantaneously. As a tech innovator, Musk's support for blockchain technologies and decentralised finance drives technological advancements and encourages the exploration of new possibilities within the crypto space.

In contrast, Donald Trump's influence is more indirect, stemming from policy decisions and regulatory frameworks that shape the long-term environment for cryptocurrencies. His administration's focus on regulation ensures that the crypto market operates within defined boundaries, promoting security and preventing financial crimes. This regulatory environment is crucial for fostering trust and stability, essential for the sustainable growth of the cryptocurrency market.

Market Sentiment and Stability

Musk's involvement often injects a degree of volatility into the cryptocurrency market. His endorsements can lead to significant price increases, creating opportunities for rapid gains. Conversely, his criticisms or concerns can cause sharp declines, posing risks for investors. This volatility, while presenting opportunities, also requires investors to stay informed and cautious about the potential for rapid market shifts.

On the other hand, Trump's regulatory stance aims to create a more stable and secure environment for cryptocurrencies. By enforcing regulations that prevent illicit activities, his policies enhance investor confidence and encourage institutional participation. This stability is vital for attracting long-term investments and ensuring that the cryptocurrency market matures responsibly and sustainably.

Elon Musk and Donald Trump play crucial, yet distinct, roles in shaping the cryptocurrency community. Musk's direct influence through investments and social media drives immediate market movements and fosters innovation, while Trump's regulatory and policy-oriented approach establishes a framework for responsible growth and security within the crypto space.

Understanding the impacts of these influential figures is essential for navigating the complexities of the cryptocurrency landscape. As the market continues to mature, the interplay between tech innovators like Musk and political leaders like Trump will remain a defining factor in the evolution of cryptocurrencies worldwide. Whether it's driving technological advancements or shaping regulatory policies, their contributions will continue to influence the trajectory of digital currencies on a global scale.

How to Invest in Bitcoin

We have reached the moment that everyone has undoubtedly been waiting for.

Here, we will look through my personal example at how and where I buy Bitcoin, and the simple methods I use to earn interest on these investments.

This is not a pyramid investment scheme, a Ponzi scheme, or any multi-level company disguised as an investment. We will also not delve into the complexities of trading, which is a skill many find challenging.

I will explain a very famous investment method that many overlook or do not pay attention to.

The idea is to outperform investment in value and also in "dividends", much like a stock. In other words, to gain from the increase in the asset's price and from holding the asset itself.

A Method to Know

The method, known by its acronym in English as **Dollar Cost Averaging**.

Dollar Cost Averaging (DCA) is the practice of gradually buying Bitcoin over an extended period of time.

Because you are purchasing Bitcoin at different times, you are likely buying it at different prices as well.

This is where the "average" comes into play.

The "average" price you are buying reflects more accurately the average price of Bitcoin over the asset's lifespan.

Examples

Scenario 1
You want to buy Bitcoin and have a total of $10,000 to invest over the entire year.

Month 1
The current price is $10,000. You decide to invest all your money now and acquire 1 Bitcoin.

Month 2
The price drops to $9,000. You have lost $1,000.

Month 3
Bitcoin rises to $11,000. You have gained a total of $1,000.

Month 4
The price falls to $8,000. You have lost a total of $2,000.
Throughout, your average acquisition price is $10,000 because $10,000 divided by 1 (purchase) is $10,000.

Scenario 2
You want to buy Bitcoin and have a total of $10,000 to invest over the entire year.

Month 1
The current price is $10,000. You decide to invest $1,000 each month, regardless of the price. So, you invest $1,000 and acquire 0.1 Bitcoin.

Month 2
The price drops to $9,000. Your average cost in dollars at this point is $9,500.

Month 3
The price rises to $11,000. You have gained a total of $1,000. You invest $1,000 and acquire 0.091 Bitcoin.
Your average cost in dollars at this moment is $10,000.

Month 4
The price falls to $8,000. You invest $1,000 and acquire 0.125 Bitcoin. Your average cost in dollars at this point is $9,500.

Lesson

The lesson you should learn from these scenarios is not that you will always achieve greater gains with this method. Anyone can create fictitious scenarios where the dollar cost averaging looks good or bad.

The point is that buying Bitcoin (or any asset, for that matter) at different prices prevents an investor from experiencing the emotional swings that occur due to short-term price volatility.

You will notice that in the second scenario, the investor is not experiencing 10% gains one month, then 20% losses the next.

Advantages

Firstly, it helps you avoid panicking when buying during major price movements. For example, if the price rises very quickly, it is often tempting to "buy in panic" and purchase at a high local price, killing your profitability. Similarly, it can be tempting to "sell in panic" during a price dip that recovers as soon as you sell.

As a trader using this method, you accept that you will buy Bitcoin at highs, but those "bad" purchases will be offset because you will also ensure you buy at lows. Therefore, there is no need to risk trying to predict Bitcoin's price movements. Instead, you can set up your investments and forget about them.

Secondly, removing all the guesswork from Bitcoin trading can also be a great benefit for mental health, as you no longer have to worry about buying low and selling high.

Lastly, dollar cost averaging tends to mitigate many of the short-term effects of price volatility.

Basically, it is for traders who are mature enough to understand that they do not know the future and do not want to rely on their own intuition when making trades.

Disadvantages

Firstly, because you make many transactions (once a week, monthly, etc.), you may incur more fees if fees are charged per operation. This can affect the profitability of your trades.

Secondly, you might miss out on gains if you are lucky and buy a large amount at a low price. That said, the goal of dollar cost averaging is to eliminate luck as much as possible from our trading strategy.

After all, luck is not a strategy; it is just a game. But we have to take the bad with the good, and for some of us, this method may mean that we will miss out on gains when it turns out we were right about that very low price we were so sure of.

Does This Method Really Work?

Dollar cost averaging is designed to eliminate short-term volatility in the portfolio's value. It is very effective at doing this.

How Is It Calculated?

To find the dollar cost averaging of your Bitcoin purchases, do the following:

Total dollars invested ÷ Total Bitcoin purchased

So, taking from the previous example, if you bought:

- $1,000 for 0.1 BTC
- $1,000 for 0.091 BTC
- $1,000 for 0.125 BTC

Then you have spent $3,000 for 0.316 BTC.

So,

$3,000 ÷ 0.316 BTC

This equals an average cost price of Bitcoin in dollars of $9,493.67. To this method, we will add the possibility of earning while we hold our Bitcoin.

My favourite Trading Strategy

One of my favourite and most effective approaches revolves around a simple yet powerful idea: buy low when no one wants to buy and sell high when everyone's caught up in the excitement. This method, rooted in patience and smart risk-taking, can help you navigate the volatile crypto market and build lasting wealth.

The Impact of Influential Figures

Elon Musk and Donald Trump have a remarkable ability to influence Bitcoin's price movements. For instance, every time Musk tweets about Bitcoin or makes a significant business move, Bitcoin's price often reacts sharply. Similarly, Trump's statements or policy changes can create ripples across the cryptocurrency market. These influences happen frequently enough that savvy traders keep a close eye on their actions to anticipate market shifts.

The Number One Rule in Trading and Building Wealth

The cornerstone of successful trading is straightforward: **buy low when others are hesitant and sell high when everyone's euphoric**. This contrarian approach leverages the natural ebb and flow of market emotions, fear and greed, to your advantage. By staying disciplined and sticking to this rule, you can make informed decisions that align with market realities rather than emotions.

Understanding the Strategy

This strategy is all about timing and psychology. Markets are driven by human emotions, fear during downturns and greed during booms. When Bitcoin's price drops significantly, fear can lead to panic selling, driving prices even lower. Conversely, during bull runs, optimism and hype can push prices to unsustainable highs. By acting against the prevailing sentiment, you can capitalize on these extreme points.

Buying Low: Seizing Opportunities

Buying low means investing in Bitcoin when the market sentiment is negative, and prices are down. This often happens during corrections or bearish trends when investors are pessimistic. For example, if Bitcoin's price falls from £30,000 to £20,000 due to negative news, it might be a prime opportunity to buy. The key here is to remain calm and confident in your analysis, trusting that the market will recover over time.

Selling High: Taking Profits

Selling high is about locking in profits when Bitcoin's price has surged and the market is in a state of euphoria. This typically occurs during bull markets when positive news and widespread optimism drive demand. For instance, if Bitcoin climbs from £20,000 to £40,000 amidst favourable regulatory developments and increased institutional adoption, it's a good time to sell. This helps you secure your gains before the inevitable market correction sets in.

The Role of Patience and Risk-Taking

Patience is crucial in this strategy. It involves waiting for the right moments to buy and sell, rather than reacting impulsively to every market movement. Successful traders understand that the market goes through cycles and that timing these cycles effectively is key to maximising returns.

Taking calculated risks is equally important. Not every downturn will lead to a rebound, and not every peak will precede a correction. Assessing the fundamentals, staying informed about market trends, and setting clear entry and exit points can help mitigate risks. This disciplined approach ensures that your decisions are based on analysis rather than emotions.

Practical Application

Let's look at a practical example to illustrate this strategy:

Scenario 1: Buying Low

Imagine Bitcoin has been on a downward trend due to negative news about regulatory crackdowns. The price drops from £30,000 to £20,000. While many investors panic and sell, you see this as an opportunity. After thorough research and analysis, you decide to buy Bitcoin at £20,000, anticipating a future recovery.

Scenario 2: Selling High

A few months later, positive news about widespread institutional adoption drives Bitcoin's price to £40,000. The market is buzzing with excitement, and prices continue to climb. Recognising the signs of market euphoria, you decide to sell your Bitcoin at £40,000, doubling your initial investment.

Avoiding Common Pitfalls

While this strategy is effective, it's not without challenges. Emotional decision-making can lead to buying too late during a downturn or selling prematurely during a surge. To avoid these pitfalls:

- **Stay Informed:** Keep up with market news and trends. Understanding what's driving price movements helps you make informed decisions.
- **Set Clear Goals:** Define your investment goals and stick to your strategy. Determine your entry and exit points in advance to avoid impulsive actions.
- **Diversify:** Don't put all your eggs in one basket. Diversifying your investments can help spread risk and protect your portfolio from significant losses.

The key to successful trading lies in disciplined execution and continuous learning. Stay patient, stay informed, and let your strategy guide you towards lasting financial success in the world of Bitcoin.

How to Stay Safe

We've all heard people refer to cryptocurrencies as scams. The reason is simple: many have lost money in crypto and ICOs by investing credibly in the wrong projects. But that doesn't mean the entire industry should be labelled as a scam! Two of the most common types of scams are ICO scams and fake trading experts or page administrators. Let's start with a brief introduction:

ICO Scams

In the cryptocurrency niche, an ICO (Initial Coin Offering) is used to raise funds for new projects and start-ups. However, this is being abused more and more. That said, I don't want to dismiss ICOs entirely. There have been enough cases where ICOs turned out to be great successes, with significant projects emerging from them.

Trading Experts

You might have come across them on social media, especially on platforms like Instagram and Twitter. They comment on crypto-related posts or send you direct messages pretending to be crypto trading experts and professional page administrators. Unfortunately, this type of scam is responsible for most of the fraud these days. Read on to learn about their methods and how you can avoid them.

ICO Scams Explained

The basic principle behind ICO scams is the same most of the time: a fake ICO is created, and extensive marketing and hype are generated to persuade people to buy in. If you don't want to fall victim to these schemes, here's what to look out for:

Too Good to Be True!

This is what all ICO scams have in common. So, before investing in any ICO, make sure to read its whitepaper, check out the team behind it, review the roadmap, and gather as much information as you can. But most importantly:

Do Your Own Research

To understand whether the offer is genuinely too good to be true or not.

Signs of ICO Fraud:
- A copied whitepaper
- Most of the team is anonymous
- An unusual rush to buy in
- Inconsistencies between what is written and what is said
- No valid reasons for the project's economic model
- No support or contact information
- No clear roadmap

Trading Experts Scams

You've definitely noticed these suspicious messages when scrolling through the comments on my profile or other crypto pages. There's not much to say about this; without a doubt, 95% of these messages lead to fraud, so please **never respond** to them.

Direct Messages on Instagram

Most of them will inform you about an investment opportunity with incredible returns. Often, they claim to have calculated how long you can earn and promise profits in a very short time. And here we go again: "If it sounds too good to be true, keep your hands off it!"

Comments on Crypto-Related Content

They'll share stories about their bad experiences and how they almost lost faith in crypto. Then, magically, a manager-influencer or a "professional" account administrator appears and helps them make immense profits effortlessly. Again, this sounds too good to be true! On the next page, you'll find some example (but real) messages from these scams.

A Personal Experience

Once, I was a victim of an online scam. It hurt because I lost a lot of money and almost gave up any online business ventures. Then I met someone who I didn't take seriously at first, but I decided to give it a try, and it turned out to be true. I traded and made my first profit – it felt like a miracle. Ready to spread the word about his good deeds, I could swear he's proven time and again that genuine managers still exist. Many thanks to him for putting smiles on my face. With a minimum of £200 and within five days after the transaction, I made a great profit of £2,400. I want you to experience financial freedom too, so contact @alexei_nikolaevich80 and you won't regret it.

I can show you how I make profits with cryptocurrency (Bitcoin) and the secret behind my successful investment. Contact me via email.

Getting Started

I recommend starting with services that have excellent mining capabilities, which help you make profits. The initial deposit to begin is £1,000 with a 10% daily return as profit.

Hopefully, this helps you identify scams. But above all, never forget the most important rule when investing: **do your own research**!

Additional Resources

Please visit my website below which you will find official links to my social media accounts.

Please join my subscribers and followers which I have over 1 million on all platforms and I am considered to be one of the most influential brands in the crypto world.

- www.mando-ct.com
- YouTube: Mando CT
- X (formerly Twitter): @xmaximist

In this community, I will provide the best of myself to bring you the latest updates, share where I am investing, discuss which platforms I am using, and who knows, maybe a few other titbits as well.

Conclusion

At this point, you might realise that something is systematically wrong with our current financial system. It's still unclear whether Bitcoin is the answer to help solve the problems that have arisen as a result of imprudent fiscal and monetary policies.

In today's context, governments around the world have been printing vast amounts of money to prevent the economy from collapsing entirely.

Major institutional investors are seeking ways to protect themselves against inflation and the devaluation of fiat currencies. Bitcoin serves as a solid hedge against these risks and could potentially be a life-changing investment for those willing to approach it with an open mind.

For the first time in history, we have the option to adopt a form of money with a limited supply, decentralised, and beyond the control of governments or banks.

An added bonus is that you have the opportunity to do so alongside Wall Street and most institutional investors.

The question is, are you ready to take this step?